Paper Oranges

Paper Oranges

CAROLYN MARIE SOUAID

George Amabile, Editor

Signature
EDITIONS

Cover design by Doowah Design.
Photo of Carolyn Marie Souaid by Michael Towe.

Acknowledgements
Grateful acknowledgement is made to the following publications in whose pages some of these poems, or versions of them, first appeared: CV2, *The Delaware Valley Poets Anthology*, *Geez Magazine*, *The Malahat Review*, *U.S. 1 Worksheets*, and *Windsor Review*. The long poem "Flight" was printed by Rubicon Press as a chapbook in 2007. "Conduit" was produced for video in 2007 by Charles-Alexandre Gagnon. "Forty Thousand Wishes on Your Birthday," "Paper Oranges," "Portrait of the Lady, Reclining, in Lingerie," and "Prisons" appeared, in previous incarnations, in *Freedom: An Anthology of Canadian Poets for Turkish Resistance* in 2006. "Road Kill" criss-crossed Montreal in 2004 as part of the Poetry-in-Motion / Poésie en mouvement (poetry on the buses) project. An earlier version of "Throat Song (Refrain)" was published in *Snow Formations* in 2002.

Thanks to Endre Farkas and George Amabile for editorial input that shaped this into a better manuscript; and to Alex, for understanding that the best distance between two points isn't always a straight line.

Some of the poems in this book were written with the financial support of the Conseil des arts et des lettres du Québec.

This book was printed on Ancient Forest Friendly paper.
Printed and bound in Canada by Marquis Book Printing Inc.

We acknowledge the support of The Canada Council for the Arts and the Manitoba Arts Council for our publishing program.

Library and Archives Canada Cataloguing in Publication

Souaid, Carolyn Marie, 1959–
        Paper oranges / Carolyn Marie Souaid.

Poems.
ISBN 978-1-897109-31-1

        I. Title.

PS8587.O87P36 2008   C811'.54   C2008-905484-9

Signature Editions
P.O. Box 206, RPO Corydon, Winnipeg, Manitoba, R3M 3S7
www.signature-editions.com

for

Adele Shaker & Paul Souaid

in memory

CONTENTS

III FLIGHT

THROAT SONG (REFRAIN)

Darkness. A tree. Dry grass husks.

Until.

Who knows how it happened, or why—
a goldfinch arrived like so much
light, puffing up his chest,

the raspberry sky
speaking mountains
through him.

And the miracle wasn't plankton
or the white tulle flounce of sea,
it wasn't God
clothed in the everyday breath of earth,

the miracle was the weight
itself, suddenly bearable.

THE WEIGHT

Everything's dead but the tree.
                    —Vladimir to Estragon

Nothing Happens, Nobody

comes, nobody goes
until absence inhales

stagnant night,
exhales frogspawn

muggy ghost-breath &
two scant bones

meagre beginnings
shaken onto the lawn,

lush, moist earth again
a second go, a throw

of dice staring up,
snake eyes spitting

out pairs:
a sun, a moon,

a man & woman
to seed the garden

LITTLE FROG LIBRETTO

we breathe we exist we subsist

carbon records the machinery
of our lives:

air-shy gestures &
      the multiple reaches of the mind

biology ticking,

      we pass each other every day
making perfunctory noise

our looked-at looks betray us

jesus bled
the river dry

we have a name for this

Morning

Air dressed in regret.
Grey, unaccompanied cloud.
The shoeless harbour.

The Graveyard Lives Inside You

You taste bone in each sip of water. News-
print, bits of the previous century, straw, musk.

Those who did or didn't make a sound when they died,
who whimpered, who trumpeted, who hit the road jack,
who refused to go gently, day or night; those

whose eyes shot forth, whose pores cried
blood, phlegm, urea, whose guillotined heads
flew, whose sponge fed the mad cow, whose
heart kissed a bullet, whose lips turned black.

You know it as Infinite dusk.

WAYS OF STAYING TOGETHER

two scripts, like versions of a screenplay:
windy Austerlitz platform, lovers gripping one another

twister, as the final train rips in, the knot unletting
them go, anchoring them

to the Left Bank, the bistro, "their" bridge

and if not Paris
                    , then Munich

after a long war and the accumulated guilt
over them, weaving its grey nest

because memories of a cattle train
and a child's grim trudge up the gangplank

on the other hand, for example

BLUEPRINT

It's not your fairy book "end" but it works:
you don't fight. You accommodate
one another's automobile.
You settle, shift into neutral,
paint the mouldings

a flat, noncommittal beige.

You wanted footings,
a man who stood tall.
You wanted to stake your ground,
wanted the comforts of home,
work, kids.

You wanted scaffolding,
crossed the boulevard for the one
with the credit card, the world view
that replicated yours.
You wanted solid brick.

WHAT SHE RECALLS OF HEAT & THE EQUATOR

flashbulb abracadabra

reddish, spasmed light &
liquid exposure

pyre, emulsion

tropical slaves welcoming
the lost soldiers of libation

apertures widened

The Unbearabale Weight of Being

God, most silent, unavailable
when you need him.

She, too, turns her back

ponders the insane root, deadly
nightshade, the hemlock,
the henbane that breedeth madness
or *slow lykeness of sleepe*

the lucky blind untied to time.

Tomorrow, she'll hang herself
with Vladimir from the tree.

How She Falls

Through the tragedy of stars—
                               theatrically.

Seeded with the push-pull attraction
of sex, a cosmos plagued
with insurmountable odds:

the glowering embers of providence
as Chance courts her other half,
dangerously, off-stage.

A familiar theme echoed through time.
The world out of joint:

blossom in a grim landscape
of men. Sky, moon, the tempting gypsy
light out of town.

Fireworks and a final,
        Shakespearean leap of the heart.

If Her Last Breath Were an Epiphany

A skewed barometer shifts
the dew point. Her eyes well up

with sabbath clouds.

She hides in the car, away
from the harping rain,

away from death.

Outside, a dozen umbrellas still
with places to go.

THE ROAD OF EXCESS

She opened the Door
            to a gust of wind

licked her blues,
she jammed with the vagrant moon

lured it, like Anaïs Nin, to her suck: secretly.

Was a decadent sign, a chink
in the armour, a tactical, syntactical shift:

love clandestine, henry miller, love as odour.

Sex leech, she boozed on the bed

danced on oil, danced hungry,
disheveled,

she danced a rough rain. Tit & ink.

Stroked until delivery.

ANACHRONISM (A PHANTASY)

gibberish, the horses you woke to

doublespeak, where tomorrow's tedious men stood

Sappho, meanwhile, lingered in the air
grassy & wanting wear

a verse in her head wheedling the moon:

two roads diverged in a yellow wood

L'intensité de l'instant

Kittens, you could be lapping
your last bowl of cream,
or toddlers on a spot of grass.
It's possible, yes.
You could be strangers
in opposite hemispheres of the globe.

Until it happens, like sticks birthing fire:
the big bang, the quantum leap.

Sure-footed, the pair of you
stepping into uncertainty
your lungs, lightweight, suffused,

ever grateful for the infinite park air.

What binds you, of course,
not the logical universe
or the reliable moon
but a common lemon desire:

Tang & verve.
The exuberant, pumped-up heart.

And finally, floating

                    within reach, grabbable
the gimme, gimme red balloons.

DADA LANDSCAPE

Look, it beckons: tambourine dawn.
A cold, queer dance.
Glaze on the naked field
where the moon slid down,
Samoan vista of mango and plum.

Follow the keys.

Swallow the jade laughter,
swallow the road.
March your bright steeds of light
to the oracle. One word,
Arcadia, will get you in.

ARBORETUM

Through secret doors of leaves,
the bright, swirled light

in & around & under

he marked her with an X
foxing the river

bull's-eyed her
right there on the spot

afterwards, wrote of apples
& full-blown trees

the heat & the hunt

they crossed a bridge & then another
on the strange road back

Daphne & Apollo

Five (Happy) Thoughts

Linden June. Decadent lawns stretch
over the silent hysteria of scent.

Desdemona capers with the moon.
Factories, disassembled, mime

summer aquarelles
or Iliad light in lemon time.

In Jakarta, parasols frolic & ferment.

IMPROVISO

First things first: we averted life.
Then we averted death, spinning

into & out, mostly out, of control.

How else explain incoherence
but for the cumulous gods sent to flatten us
on the freeway?

We shot past the manic snow
to our february hacienda.
My feet were ice. The bed was night.

Somewhere between heaven & hell
we rode the squall, swirling

swerving. Just this side of light.

AFTER HIS SCENT, WHAT?

His hands. Not the gashed, beaten
palms of the felon who suckled her
on underground tales of a Cuban jail.

This one, with his hands, kept tabs.
In Venice, and in parked cars

in the alleys
of night's unmarked roads.

Each of her married years
a digit, moonlit, on his hands.

Whose Hands

Whose elfin, underpaid hands
turned tricks from the Third World

into the haute couture
of the civilized West; whose hands

spun cloth lighter than breath
finer than a sparrow's nest

whose hands sewed ignorantly
day and night

threading ambivalence into the air
adulterous impulses

whose hands I dreamt only once
in passing

because more drawn to the delicate
awakening of snow

whose phantom hands whispered
think, pause, on second thought
return the merchandise

RETURN THE MERCHANDISE

whose virtuous hands assembled
a plain, coin-toss ultimatum

pack light, leave word, return
the merchandise

SKATING

You know "the skate" like a bad dream,
his touching you in the back seat
of a car, dashboard retired
& always ranging
outside the aperture

your wayward, jezebel name
way off the radar, wavering
already because of hers
in black & white, focused,
holding on

because of her small feet
steady on the ice, because of her
wifely hand in another afternoon,
no—*years* of afternoons,
tugging him back.

THE WAIT

How to unwind when the canvas is wrong,
when beaches and stretches
of pastel impressionism don't fit the frame?

Dawn lingers between your walls
like driftwood in the wrong shade of sleep.

Nesting light, though comforting,
is in a repeat sky,

the whaling sea spray, elusive.
What you perceive as the moon dangling
from a slim branch is only aspirin.

Pointless to stay in bed, count sheep
or imagine a clean slate

when Friday is on a return flight to Monday
and the 4 a.m. crows just won't stay away.

RIFF

Jazz on the brain, he type mood
& january blue.

Blunt mud notes from the gut.
Insomniac man.

Writing make him hot, make play
make dance on the page.

Put wild cunt sway in the air.
Absent, even, she there.

Rain Rain

Rain in the lilac. Rain
off the split white birch.
Pecking rain. Rain
in the garbage.

Forty days & forty nights.

Rain on all species, visible &
invisible. The saved & the unsaved.
Dog-shake, flyaway rain. Pearl rain.
Rain on the moon.

Mauve, missing-him rain
in her hair.

INERTIA

CONDUIT

On Monday you're here, by Friday you're pressed into foil
and auctioned for scrap. Meanwhile, the Earth
spins on, without you.

There's a soothing way to read this,
metaphors to lullaby the gloom—

       tranquil room of syringes and washcloths.
Things floating along just fine
'til afternoon shifts its weight
to the other leg.

Imagine a weak signal, then nothing.

You're in a broom closet, blindfolded.
You have a dormant view of the parking lot.
Impenetrable light
separates you from the millions
of other pixels stored and waiting in databases.
It is a curse.

It is a blessing.
The city that grew inside you is gone.
So are the spooks and secret police.
All the encryption devices.
An entire broadband network—erased.
The streets are deserted, you should be relieved.
No more waiting around for text messages.
You're a free man, free of the ugly
and the uglier, war machines and mass graves,
lipgloss, Viagara. No more buzz
in the frontal lobes
about holocausts and malign gods.

No more music, including the *Goldberg Variations*.
Eyes brushed shut, you don't even dream these things:
hatching daylight, the faces of your own offspring.

All you can do you've already done,
folding yourself back into the moth, into darkness
nothing to say anymore, and saying it.

Post-Traumatic Stress Disorder

Your childhood fear of barking dogs
nags like a low-grade headache.
Free will and a weak set of batteries keep it going.

Some Thursday, mid-month, it occurs to you
that you're a nobody, an insignificant.
You go to night school, hoping for tools
to manage your dread
which now has a textbook name:

objectless anxiety.

Homework is the same each class:
create a story, something
to give heft to your life, stability.

The world becomes coherent.
You play the part of a man,
paint a picturesque village, hills,
Christmas snow.

One day, the clouds above your home
disassemble into weapons of mass destruction.

STUCK IN TRAFFIC, LISTENING TO A YULETIDE MESSAGE OF THE EMERGENCY BROADCAST SYSTEM

Take Pi to a billion decimal places and we're still
adding to the string. Events in geologic time now occur
in the eyeblink of a human life.

We're waiting for the Answer.

Years ago, seventy thousand or so, ice sheets
moved across America, forever altering the Earth.
We're a paranoid nation on the wrong bandwidth,
fearful of Armageddon
and the suspected terrorists in our ovaries.

We obsess over pattern and causality,
read cancer into the white painted lines of the road:
zero point zero zero
zero zero—do you understand?

No matter what, southbound is a bad bet.

Tomorrow, stay put.
Throw some logs into the fire.

Dream your little dreams of the giftwrapped Hand
guiding the kingdom to its perfect end.

PRISONS

1

Nothing is more benign than a greeting card,
except, perhaps, a suburb
of butterfly sprinklers and imperceptible waste.
I'm thinking of mine. Of all things,
our immaculate holding cell won awards.

And except in our overblown Bonnie & Clyde
imagination, except on our wildest days,
we never called it "jail"
because, truth be known,
it was less death camp than military base,
matchbox of disciplined living
behind bars: basic plumbing
and a simple fumigated cot.

Year after year, the V-shaped guard running the tour
hammered the same old maxims
about keeping our head screwed on,
our nose to the grindstone,
lest we end up like *him*, and here,
darkness would break across his face
summoning Zeus,
his brow, a sinister streak of lightning
lighting that mythical dip in the floor
where an inmate's sorry spook
lay flattened like a phone book
and he'd pause, briefly, while the kids
ran a hand back and forth
over the spot, feeling for the twitter
of a soul, a clue, a last regret,
because once upon a time
convicts, too, had pure hearts.

2

The imagined is worse than anything real
is what I thought, until Argentina
          consummate Mother of Understatement
served up the best of the Jewish ovens,
the subtlest Chinese water drip
to the hardened few
bleeding rations from the same small rat.

And when justice finally crawled
into *The Jail at the End of the World*
there was always *Unit 29*

where, an hour a day, men escaped
the sour emissions of their groin
forced out of the minuscule dark
to meet the imperial light

the afternoon braise
a more "civilized" stoning

according to sources.

3

There are no names, no lives beyond this point.
There are no wives, no children to be liquidated
in the anonymous, cloak-and-dagger night.

Questions are a burden, though sometimes, word sneaks in
through a slot in the brick,
up three dark flights to where death lingers
in every green beret of the Party's "fallen flowers"

martyred to the wall. Another rose, radiant
and in full bloom, welcomes you:

Your Canadian luggage looks heavy.
Code for "You'll surely take a cab to the Revolution."

Maybe you are dreaming this. Maybe it's the grog
of centuries percolating underfoot, or the mice

inside your brain working on you, implicating
you in her slippery confession
about the comrade in her bed, his hands

issuing orders on how to move for him,
how to dress, how to bend into and out of the light
because he's the sun

she will always rise to, unconditionally.

What Could Happen

trust the hamlet hemmed in green
trust the covered nest & august drinks
on your perfect lawn

better this
than the frayed horizon
the ambiguous trees
nothing to hang your hat on
as the distant bell
goes off in your head
some thursday
when you find yourself
picking at a stray thread
on your sleeve
the tailored light
about to unravel, taking you
to an undefined place
in the heart: a hell
for which there is no word
no cordoned-off grass

just a territorial wind
that would rip the roof
off your life
dashing the circuitry
the dog the kids
in a tangled orbit

avalanching

CLARITY

The plane is booked; the cruise, as well.
You've made an appointment
for your hair and nails.
Wisely, you took additional health coverage,
you can never be sure
on foreign turf. All those *turistas* on deck
with clever accents, any one of whom
might have a gun in his luggage.

You're in pajamas planning the day
when an envelope arrives with your divorce.
Verbatim what you'd told the judge,
but the words tumble out all wrong.
You navigate, colliding with the same muck
over and over. Your blood pressure shoots up.
The cat jumps down. Any time now,
you could have a seizure.

Your god says it's about surrender,
letting the breath flower
                    unsystemically—
The garden is an accident of the mind.
What it makes of all the gibberish
growing chaotically from seed.

Meaning has arms and legs, a face.
It is ugly, it is beautiful.
Which it is, you'll never be sure.

In a downtown club, a man yells
Turn on the lights!
But what he really wants is full disclosure:
Who got the house, the car, the kids?
Who accidentally got creamed by a bus?

Keep it up, you'll begin to sound like *him*.

What I Might Say at the Vernissage

Don't ask about my obsession with doors.
Doors endorsing God, sin, *chocolatine*.
Weathered-but-still-standing doors,
the paint worn thin.

Don't ask how it's done, how a photographer
shoots from the sidelines,
how the pixels of his mind add up to a perfect view
of those who risk calamity
entering doors.

Up ahead, hugging the road, an Asian
and her toppling empire of laundry.

What, you ask, could I possibly know
about her modest feet, minuscule
rice paddies hastening her along
the broken cement,
her birdwalk tenacity
no match for the continental
divide? Me, the reticent one.

Of course, I could lie

follow the oversized January coat
that is all her, bigger than her
into the laundromat

her bold, miniature frame
crossing the threshold
into vapours and cloud
as though she (we) were walking
through the great, open door
of the sky.

I could tell you the mice inside
never bothered me a bit.

But truth hovers somewhere
between the shadowy interiors
of mysterious places
and the masochist in me

      safely out of range, making do

with the camera around his neck
and the familiar, focused light of day.

CITY SANDALS

Your myth of Identity was a return to darkness.
I tell you this for your own good.
Things matter, including the most inconsequential:
Glaze on a pear or a small burning bush.
The engine of a snowflake.
On a silver platter, I gave you material.

too much?

But you who could never see
that images were merely openings,
made it your life's work to shatter the light.

Adrift and wandering, you preferred rooms,
cups to contain your tempermental stars.
You forced consciousness across my coronal sky,
became a ruthless arbiter of time—
but for what?

Appleseeds have gone haywire.
Morning wails from her toxic roots.

There is only one pilgrimage: the infinite
roars at tens of millions of degrees.
It overloads powerlines, disables navigation.

Vehemently.

VAN GOGH'S CHAIR

Migraines migrate west
      across my head

criss-crossing streets
of congenital heat,

clusters of fruit and fleas
and the whirring industry

of dust. Stress factors in,
lopsided thoughts of yellow

Paris smog. Woke up again
with Van Gogh's chair
on the brain.

PAPER ORANGES

You're trapped in the cage,
the weather, life, against you:
sleet's ermine shawl,
groundhogs making meat
of your pumpkin. It's defeat
everywhere you look:
lean muskrat gardens, graveyards
of mangled sinks and telephones.
Not once, but twice, you mistook
your son for an iPod.

You're desperate to believe in God
but what inhabits you, locked
behind a chain-link fence
is the blinkety-blank road,
the same slovenly dog
mutating into something bigger
and uglier each day
hoarding the inadequate light.

You long to wake up just once
with an original thought
in your head, an image,
some beautiful impossibility

: paper oranges.

MAD RIVER

Whatever else, poetry is freedom.
—Irving Layton

The water spoke, unevenly.
Two voices, in tandem.

One grim & hooked
at the mouth. The other

pure, unimpeded
salamander,

a joyous leap
of the tongue.

When you haven't done
freedom in awhile

you forget
what it sounds like.

aphoristic

FORTY THOUSAND WISHES ON YOUR BIRTHDAY

To be universal, to be the scandalous
burn-your-bra snarl in the yard:
jungle of exploded pollen

to take the blushing, grenadine moon
in your mouth

to stroke the velvet, vulva harps
of girls, to watch men
watch you in violet desire

to map Equador on your belly
to rub your bullet wounds
with spiders and arsenic

to lie porous in a capricorn sarcophagus

amorous Morning at the foot of your bed,
brushing her hair.

BREAST, SKY, LIGHT

For my birthday, half-measures
half-smiles, half-light, half
a heart: this morning

you were neither here
nor there, lost
in *anothersphere*
while I touched you in bed;

whereas, a night ago
under the full moon
your firm hand on my breast said

Look at the goddess
and make your wish.

And from the gravel roof
beneath our feet
spread the sky

and below the sky
the whole naked world
burned like a million candles.

FOR WALT, FRANK ET AL, IN MEMORIAM

My telescopic brain once marvelled
at the rambling expanse—

philosophers, especially. The Sistine Chapel.
Our planet's galactic contentions.

You'll forgive me saying I overextended myself.

These days, I'm rather fond of inertia,
my personal hill of toenail clippings.

And today, well, I'd kill for a microscope.
Look in on myself a thousand times enlarged,
rippling the greatness of a smaller pond.

My eloquent heart like a frog in mud
belting the thrill of itself, the eye
of a .38 staring it down.

Think of it.

Whose Design, whose god even comes close
to a long, short drop from the sky?

FIGURE ASCENDING

I've no idea whose life this is
or why the soft spot for a few thick clouds
and nameless blooms
that stirred me awake last spring
through a ripped-up screen

And now yes, that I mention it

further signs—
footprints, handprints
in the field,
weeks of worm-fed rain
upon the squelch through which

a morning mist would someday rise.

FGHT DPOR CY

The days those days were a brown scroll
of paper towel and missives on mugs
in factory lunchrooms across the nation

never mind the soap dispensers made in China,
nothing working right anymore.

A piped-in message, largely ignored,
made a brave return, later, in a fortune cookie:

Change your perspective, it said.
Activate Imagination's alphabet.

First, I worried about a wrong move
wreaking havoc at the Pentagon,
a monday war

but even the masses
with their dull mind understood
there are no coincidences.

Letters on my coffee cup joined in solidarity,
issuing proclamations: Fight the Diaspora

Send in a Bright Battalion of Oranges
Puncture the Armour of Kitchens and Knives

Hang a New White Bulb over the City.

ROAD KILL

I never meant to run you down.
Frighten, yes.

Coming at you
in my wolverine dress & heels, aiming
dead on
as your slow wit
bellied unsuccessfully for the ditch.

Nix the swerving car, the impact,
hysteria, & what's left is pure

unadulterated desire: my imprint on your wool.

Skid marks & the wet sound of you,
oozing.

Let's Put the Gun in Our Hands

Am I allowed to write that I would like to hunt down
George W. Bush, the president of the United States,
and kill him with my bare hands?
              —Ben Metcalf, *Harper's Magazine*, June 2006

Let's wave the flag, once, for the record.
Let's show some initiative.
Let's stare down the cold, ugly barrel.
Let's pray.
Let's pull the legs off every neuron
              and revel in the fireworks.
Let's shoot first, and never ask why.
Let's dance with the smoking gun in our hand.
Let's powder the air with the Fourth of July.

My Tahiti

I'll know when to pack up and call it a life.
Plumbing the depths of my January cocoon
I'll do it in style, in my best summer whites.
Don't expect it to be a Saturday night,
it might be midweek, say Tuesday
in a raging snowstorm. Instinct will tell me
the time has come to put it away
in the bottom drawer with my winter wools.
A bright blue package will arrive with an invitation
to comb the dumpster for my island paradise—
ferns and wild banana trees, beatnik fauna.
Coconuts growing sideways beneath the lucid stars.
I'll pour a flute of pomegranate wine,
watch *Casablanca* one last time.
The room adrift, the mind bathed
in Gauguin's aquarium light.

On the runway, a plane will be waiting.

FLIGHT

Mazel Tov

Civilization went from a kiss to a village to a stone field
while we sat distracted by an orangutan
and his monkey affiliates.

"Erudite" humans, we wondered after the fact.
How? Where was I?
How did Tuesday put Wednesday on high alert
without our ever realizing it?
Were we busy watching all-night sports?

It was November,
yam season, most of us napping
in the generous lap of the gods.
All afternoon, snowflakes listened
while rats in their quiet dens grew brains.

Shots fired, the celery flew.
Sunlight thawed an entire island
of oysters and bread.
Sure it was a party, a celebration, but then—

The good news is good news, of course,
practical tips on how to replant:
Once daily, kiss an apple.
In case of injured ova, make salt.

Sing as though the sky were a bowl of oranges.

Vita Nova

It wasn't meaningless.
You weren't a speck in an alien universe
of rusted car parts and broken stoves,
briefly suspended between north and south,
birth and death,
a handful of short-lived gifts in between:
glistening dawn. Woodsmoke and autumn leaves.
Pleasure followed by acute pain
then utter incomprehensible annihilation.
It wasn't that.
It was days of ordinary days,
walking by the same wrecking ball on my way
to the same garbage dump, days and days
of reality TV and unresolved wars
until another day,
when inadvertently I took a wrong turn and found myself
in an invisible field of electricity and circuit boards,
this one opening into that, and another,
and another, for as far as the naked eye could see.
Feeding but also obliterating the static horizon.
No, it wasn't a dream. It was a gentle tug at my sleeve,
a young girl in a summer dress
saying "come" with her eyes,
pointing at something I couldn't grasp,
something way in the distance
and I could tell by the tingling in my hands and feet,
by the hair standing up on the nape of my neck
that the dormant butterflies of earth
were readying themselves for lift-off.

New Year's Day 00:01 A.M.

Dropped, the Ball orchestrated the Big Bang,
the constellations, the Square
& its ear-nose-and-throat-splitting invective.

Night effervesced. Then it was done.

Earth blackened on her molten stick.
Ancient cities dwindled into coals.

One by one, the lights went,

popping until the filament of the last bulb
spittled & singed its comet tail.

Not done—I was wrong.
An icicle leapt.

Plenitude crept into the congealed
circuitry of my blood.

Pine boughs laced with snow
whispered your name.

POINT OF NO RETURN

You're at that point on the journey, familiarity
waning with every click of the speedometer.
You no longer know which negligible
pile of brick is actually your old house.
It could take days to find your way back,
despite the elastic light. The spaniel you left
pattering in the sprinkler
might as well be dead for all he remembers you.
It takes all your oomph just to call him,
and even then, his name catches in your throat
like a small burr, gets belligerent
with the wind, jousting a little
before getting sucked under your Michelins.
Through the rearview mirror,
you're suddenly aware of firewood
jumping off your truck, a couple
of grey canisters, your old man's tackle.
You don't even care
that you are swerving. What was once a dot
on the map is now less than an afterthought,
a box of spare parts
banging together in the dark:
your neglected porch swing, a moth angry
with its light bulb. Right now,
the instant is all you know: the sun
breaking out, contented fieldstone.
An elm in the distance, springing new growth.
The secret is not looking back.

ASLEEP / AWAKE

...unlike the ivy, I die if I attach myself.
—André Breton

The light has changed, though it's ill-advised to say
this is summer, this is winter.
True enough, there are burial pits
where men have gone from pink to black
in the eyeblink that history calls "eons."

Your father, like fathers past, will die.

Knowing this, acting on instinct,
the bird inside you, sad and frightened of change,
seeks solace in the natural world:
clustered hills, the solid horizon.

The good news is the Continuum, what is best understood
by allowing the universe to expand.

Seasons bleed into one another.
People pass from hospital bed into Spirit,
sometimes painfully.

In England, archaeologists excavated shards
of criminals, mostly young men,
executed four centuries ago: bits of a twelve-year-old
hanged and buried face down in a moat, another
whose skeletal fist
held the last black stump of a cross.
Also, two sawn-off crania, minus
the skulls they were once attached to.

By all accounts, the sun returned
and the lilacs, it seems, opened anyway.

MORE THAN A HAIR
—for Artie Gold

Take the elastic medley of your name—
the skin stretches in spite of my short-lived brain
&   later, much,   round & round it will go
                            the best vinyl record of the times

            I hardly knew you, but for a phone call once

from the ER, where panic flew
& for a beat, I shelved the typeset bones of your life
gathering mites in the book-filled crates
of a mouldy shop, several shops

                coherence from you, above all, above
the ceremony of x-ray machines & hissing syringes,
your brief on how to help a friend
prone to losing things trace a way from the car
back to his missing key

the abbreviated cosmos in under a minute
complete in a coffee spoon, in the shrinking light
through a coin booth:
your final beautiful chemical waltz
just days before you checked out.

Note To Self

Study epitaphs for future reference
but definitely not on rainy days:
the lines and lines between lines
are almost always blurred
if not washed up altogether. Forget
verse or a dead man's clever aphorisms
smudged with time, go for the unambiguous
arsenal of bullets, the succinct uni-
verse of your life
because you get a good clear sense of the guy
who claims that minerals were his love
or chemistry or seashells or older women, no—
sex with older women. Guthrie.
Murder ballads. The alkaloids.

Can't you just picture him?
Sullen. A little rough
around the edges, his day-old scruff
sprouting up from behind a good book.
Burroughs, of course. Or Chandler.
All of the above.

P.S. No matter what, shoot from the hip.

Flight

I

       DIVESTING YOURSELF, you fly up and out, seated
and snapped inside the winged capsule

              immensity ahead,

a way to forget what mirrors at home
keep reminding you of

6 a.m. buzzer jettisoned you,

Samsonite hunched by the door
stuffed with the kitchen sink.
Gift-wrapped: truffles, tisane,
books about your city

you desiring clarity, an unburdening
of the past. You could lose your self,

reinvent yourself in this country.

The pudding of clouds embracing you.

2

Good Common Sense From Home—

Viscose is a flash in the pan. Think "natural" fibres:
cotton, linen. December wools.

In Québec: scarves, long johns, *pure laine*.

Use Javel.
Laundromats breed staph infection.

Be discriminating, pragmatic. A city is a city
is a city. Stay home and raise a family.

Remember this: safety in numbers.

Keep aphids out of the garden.
You reap what you sow.

Nothing in this world is accidental.
God can't be wrong.

3

But at the Other End of the Spectrum—

Sage advice from P.K. Page
short, succinct
                —*always be bold*

You took it as a sign—how could you not?
Unconnecting the connected dots
of your life, short-circuiting
the mainframe until all that's left

of "truth" is the pixellated memory,
a poacher's target shot up with holes—

the forest imperceptible in the trees

shape without form, shade without colour

the great, boiled oceans
before Gutenberg
and the ascending major scales

chaos drifting in a prehistoric egg

4

VERTIGO, moments after take-off.

City-swill of crosses and cathedrals at your window
forcing open and shut
the tiny portal of your throat.

You left without goodbyes, without a spit
or a handshake. Cushioned between your ears,
a few, resonant words from the folks:

The news is not your friend.
Believe half of what you read.

There were never six million.

Beware. He'll arrive like Lucifer in the night.
Confiscating a big, gullible piece of your life.

5

PRAIRIES FROM 12,000 FEET:
Teal and ochre stretch of Provence.

Easily misconstrued for a straw-weave mat
or a disciplined cross stitch of harvest
and pond. Lucid, you sense the pieces

don't fit, you glimpse the magnified braid
of their lives, all that bristle and shag
rubbing them the wrong way.

Beyond maize: the brown, nettled land.
Arid, contorted earth heaving upward,
frissoning the hairs along your neck.

You smell the ironed aprons of women
in their Mennonite homes
sticking Post-Its to the refrigerator.
Tuesday's list by the Ten Commandments:
Splurge on something red and slinky.
Go for broke. Picture a plane, Paris.
Flirt waywardly
with the men in the grocery aisle.

Even at this altitude,
you smell the unspeakable drought.

6

FROM THE COCKPIT, a plea for seatbelts
as your pilot drowns in a maelstrom
of thought. Fumbling to articulate the mushroom
you're entering. A simple cloud. And yet.

Poet, you understand the slither of words,
your dictionary slick with nuance: *pewter, gunmetal, haze.*
And all those subtleties of "white."
      —vanilla, oyster, pearl. Bechamel.

Why stop there?
The intellect knows a cloud is only one hue
bleeding into the next: *sea-foam, alabaster, camel.*

Your mother would see it otherwise.

Like that simple afternoon in the park when she flew
her happy kite, you sulking in your upright pram.
Small but defiant for the first time.

You've heard it at every family gathering since.
How breathlessly she ran from thing to thing
christening each with the perfect word.
How she pointed to the cloud above your head
and pursed her lips, eager for you to get it right.

No, Baby, not grey, she mouthed. *White.*

Say it. White.

7

MIDFLIGHT, you snooze
through an even band of galactic light.

Until turbulence: electroshock's
shrieking comet through your blood.

For every action, planetary reaction.

The necessary disturbance
of bones. You with your pick

of tragedy. Bomb shard from Baghdad.
Lightning streaks of human pith

radiating from the Towers. America,
in collusion, on the corporate fence.

The grotty, unsavoury little nations
excommunicated. The final toll in *stuff*:

broomsticks and ruby red slippers.
Israel, Lebanon, decimal dust.

Jolted awake, it occurs to you that
you can *never go home.*

8

You Left The Coda, En Route.
Somewhere over Thunder Bay.
A significant piece of the fiction.

No, you left it at home
in a bottom drawer, layered
in the onion-skins of your notebook.

Actually, that's not true either.

A question of self-preservation, you buried
most of the evidence.

It's about being smaller than you pretend to be.
It's about hiding, about the huge impropriety
of mixing blood with "the enemy"
and then turning, ambivalently, against him.
It's about the pills you take to fall sleep,
wake up, stop crying, start eating again.

It's about moping around, listening
to cello music. It's about therapists,
the insanity of wanting his babies
and wanting them dead—too.

It's about your family saying
            he's all wrong for you.
It's about wanting him back
yet wanting him out.

It's about realignment, an ear to the angels
mouthing goodbye.

9

Once, Your Mother's World Went Awry.
In her own backyard.

Though she rarely mentions it, except to say:
When I had my problem.

First, caterpillars in the magnolia.
Before long, a dubious bloom on her ovary.

Nothing, in fact,
next to the silenced chrysalis of Race.

Hail Mary, full of grace, she said.
Hail Mary, full of grace, her mother said.
Hail Mary, full of grace, her mother's mother echoed

from beyond the grave.

10

You Expected Orderly White Wheatfields, Not Dreadlocks.

Certainly not these tantalizing,
African yellows. Nor totems and tom-toms
teasing up a storm.

Welcome to Calgary.
Kudos to Tristan Tzara who said
logic is always wrong.

Who might well have said
things are never what they seem
from 40,000 feet.

Some are diminished
by the austerity of circumstance.

One life, you're in an adrenalin crowd
boarding a plane,

the next, you're a number
on the Zero train

to dust.

Most Diminishment Slips in Under the Radar:

The disparate, desperate lives of men
glorified in the news, or embedded
in the bland porridge of elevator music.
Forever the black death shawls

out of sight, out of mind.

The plain white bread you ate religiously for years
secured your place in the Lego world
of homes and gardens.

Until the "unpredictable," relegating you
to a speck:

from a deep valley, the arctic screech.
Snowy owl in her final, emphatic
descent.

The Rockies, suddenly demonic
at your window.

A staggering tour de force
upending you.

12

JETLAGGED IN VICTORIA, delirious,
you feel your own strength blossoming,
or at least a renaissance.

It might have been the Garry oaks
and their immense network of limbs.
It might have been the solid, wrought iron gates
grounding you. The Nootka rosehip.

It might have been the mapping
of all these textures onto each other:
clay, stucco, the finest Edwardian moss.

You could go on like this, growing your list.
Because it energizes, reminds you
how good it feels to have life
close to the skin:

leaf-splat against the corky bark.
Green herringbone lawns. Underfoot,
a carpet of chestnuts.

13

Hours Later, an unfamiliar night.
Sweetened by the cascading herbs
and the clear, unembellished senses.

Gone are all the anonymous dead, the multitudes
in their cold, whiskery graves.

What seduces, instead: the visceral singularity.
Your verboten Jew-boy from another time,
that nefarious blood defining him. He, too,

gazing through a thatched roof
at this same harvest moon.

Somewhere.

It's your turn and you are willing.
Among the Chosen few,
you channel God, huge and resplendent,
into the malleable core of the planet.

Etrog, myrtle, willow, palm.
East, west, north, south,
you give the sacred wand
a spectacular shake.

You picture Moses in the desert,
sip some hot stone soup,

you let the sky become a blanket
over both of you.

14

WHAT YOUR HOST REVEALS, wistfully
about her garden.

That the frail, smallish bush is *pyrocantha*.
Apologies for the family home
diverting the sun.

Further up the street, you meet the same berries
in stunning fall coats.
Some yellow, some red. Profuse.

Greys at the food stand, including pumpkins,
unremarkable. Given the exuberant foreground:

second-hand book in your bag,
its blushing jacket water-stained.
Paradise Regained.

The one true thing: this urgency of fruit.
A million and one possibilities.
How easily the berries travel
from his mouth to yours,
yours to his.

By simply imagining it.

LEVITY: A STUDY

Exposed to high temperatures
chemical baths
      & gamma rays

phantom lovers

finger rainbow light
through the
      sedentary wool of fog;

lift to become breath

or

the kiss-and-tell plumage
of flyaway snow.

After the Hijab

octopal joy, o jazz

      crow the breeze, i'm on the rag

pep my signal, o haifa-dad
      spirit me your bandy pip

ax-groom, yaqui-taster
break the dye

      parade as nectar my forest-red tip

o happy airdrops

      thrillingly mosaic

—*ARREST me!*

I Love You

orangutang you said
and my heart,
       washed & ironed
wired for an honest day's work
jumped to attend

wrestling the primate
into citrus halves
on the floor

a monkey blend
of yin & yang—

pure, unmitigated light

i thought you said
the other thing

the way the sudden sun
just leapt out of nowhere

PORTRAIT OF THE LADY, RECLINING, IN LINGERIE

A bloated, afterwards morning
in bed. She, greedy as a beet
in juice, with a need

for the enormity of living,
touching, tasting, smelling
to fatten her plait. The knot lingers,
swells, strand by strand
she dissolves,

vanishes through the open screen
to become pelvic Chagall light,
more indolent than pink. Invasive.
Into the birdless sky, a rayed
declaration of self.

Nothing exists beyond love
it decides, and if the warmed
polar ice wants to piss
on the world, then let it.

THE PROGRAM

It builds slowly, this theory of loss. Before words,
before the fetal brain shuts its door on the sky—

You fix a point in space: the "object" of your love.

You let them feed you from the lectern all their talk
about the seasons, the necessary rotation of the planets,
you understand if unconditionally it returns,
this object of your affection, then it's yours for the keeping.

You fall asleep, dreaming
not of the inordinate strain it will take to stay afloat
but of the besotted prince at the end of the line.

For a time, summer stops coming.

You withdraw, taking what you think belongs to you:
woolens and tweeds,
all the old leaves hugged close to the heart.
They become memories, but of what—colour?

If, decidedly, he refuses you
you want the world to shut up about it
want the birds to take flight, the sun on its hind legs
to disappear, finally

or not so finally: the way of the golden daffodil
wilting into sage beginnings.

AFTERWORD

Closer to death, we become Earth sipping the dregs
in her bottom drawer: soup bowl of doddering swans, the last sour grapes
from a vine. Seven days of zilch, seven of hypothermia.
This is how we wait, semi-alert, frost setting in while the rats
grind their diamond teeth into glass. Windows once heralded spring;
now make vows they can no longer keep. Stars extinct, art extinct,
the need to turn centuries of children (ransacking garbage)
into a fairy tale has dwindled into the spoiled night.
The world is tired.

But I, with ink and a small pad, wan and weak, would still write
a singing epilogue, a postscript in memoriam.
Friend, I might say. Notice the moon straddling a tear
while the salt sea, born this late into jail and starved for water, beckons.
Treasure the quelled trees, the dry wharf split in half.
Man has slipped and fallen once or twice,
but still with the birds he rises at dawn.
Think. Where would we be without drive, without verve,
this moored light waiting in the heart?

AFTER THE CREMATORIUM

La beauté sera CONVULSIVE *ou ne sera pas.*
—André Breton

The morning of the crematorium
I awoke,
seasons of the palest branch
within reach
my face, in sleep,
having pushed into your autumn hair
lips first, then a cheek, an ear
these being your finest days, here
for a last leap &
we twined & moved into one another
as though it were the first time, the last
your neck smelling faintly of ovens & ash
the telephone springing with news
of the crematorium & directions
on how to get there.

Lured away, disconnected
you brushed past with your hair
or this indigo thought
of your hair in my mouth

left talking messages to yourself
notes & grocery lists
pinned to the refrigerator

as though order would beget order
laid it all out for me, later
on Post-Its:

Short & sweet at the crematorium,
you'd say. One minute he was here, the next—

In fact, a painfully slow braise.

Hours wedged in the jaws of a "whale"
strand by strand, released,

the body unfurling like ribbon.

That afternoon as he cooled into winter light,
Chet Baker from the stereo
fogged up your window.

I floated in your dozing arms
above the february freeze,
my inner trumpet building
to springtime's leggy fields

to Giverny, where
              blooming, blossomed, I ran
carrying what I'd been carrying around
all these months
the huge box that is not a box
but the love that is always you
all gauze & gossamer

fluid as a jazz trail, as a bedouin song
lifting in death—

"Drift blue" or LIVE without any chance
of parole, without wings, get lost, go beyond
the warmth of down
move into each other's mythical sun,
crown it in your palm & cherish.

Then, drumbeat, the unmentionable,
gloom & doom, Chet—oh yes,
the real showstopper.

No one said, but we all knew
about the heroin in your blood
the morning that smashed across your balcony
when hope entered my left ear
a city coming straight for me
your estranged voice in all that sharded light
plunging me into the caves of my own dawn
where a piano still played
&
I couldn't help fondling that solemn place
because I had with me the seeds
of that greater package,
a few yellow notes in my hand
chirping down through the clouds.

All I ever wanted to do was become light.

Voices small & heard
        on the day of my birth:
low distant hills sending up signals,
quivering notes of brass & fire.

I remember the solid road
with my walking stick & a good pair of shoes
until unexpectedly the earth gave way
the great plates shifting underfoot
& upward I shot into the sky
agitating the clouds

        clamouring, clamouring

as though the next moments
for someone else utterly depended on it
& now, well, now…

I spilled the hopelessness of "blue"
said you must feel it, too, but—
I stopped
half expecting you to say it first:
how the sun has learned from me its rays, its intensity
the way I arch my back
for the sheer pleasure.

And whether you went down on me
then & there
or in the wicks of your eyes
you were telling me with your telling look
that you loved my glow
how I radiate happiness
how the idea of my hands
around that sacred box
strings you along
how when it finds its way
all this mantled love
into the most unnameable parts of you
it is merely a hand
needing to be where it is needed.

Secrets: I know humming rooms
louder than the average brain, I have keys
I know tedium & the slog of drifting
backwards through time

that God goes and changes the record on us is slog
that Chet got cut off before the end is slog
that still you're not home is slog, too
slog was even slog all those hours ago
at the crematorium, hours ago
in bed before anything

before the telephone woke us up
before the radio woke us up
before thoughts of becoming
bags of dust woke us up
before the generator went on
before the lights went on

when all signs of the day
pointed to more
than a dull grey walk through the snow.

9 o'clock, where are you? Why resist a lithe wine
on the tongue, the firmest purple grape?

I despise my slow demise,
the sloth of apartment clocks
reminding me reminding me reminding me
of my ticking cells that expire with the wait

nothing changes my skin needing your scent
my breath needing your eyes
I drink you especially, especially
when you're Lost.

What urge beyond magnetic pull?
What secret, interstellar code among souls?

       An enigma unsolvable:

the chemistry of leaf & leaf
rubbing up against love

wet & wet

Knowing all this,
how are stillness & death viable choices?

Isn't the point that jittery uncertainty
when blade nicks skin
the very first time
when the man, larger-than-life,
dips his heart in an unfamiliar scent?

Isn't it about the purity of risk?

Once your hot sweet nest
is laced with the run-off melt
the dew from him nearing you

once you taste, once you smell
the weight of him
you'll not turn your back
on the lusty stars

you'll never say no
to the candy of earth.

What greater gift than snow on snow,
a tenor sax, the electric charge before you enter
a room, the door about to speak,
the atoms unstable,
dangerously unmaking themselves

                helixing

into a staircase of bugled light
opened to the cosmos
the balloon of Man, ascending.

Both of us there, beyond ourselves
orbiting the outermost limits of skin.

It overflows the cup, spills outward
across the continents,
flooding the immensity of earth: this want

for small trembling voices when *he touches her.*

But when finally he deserts her
         (and he will) once & for all
taking with him
the airbrushed fields
the afternoon around her heart

     what then?

She can't, won't imagine
walking hand in hand
with the turtle days of august,
the arrested trees

loses herself, for now,
in the poem:

I am the black wedding apple
I am not the fish you meant to catch
do not throw me back,
savour the worms
sprouting blithely from within.

What if you were really gone?

I pictured this as you waved goodbye
at the ovens, mask weighing down
"saying" in your own mute way

stoic on the outside, tenderly within
where a thin grass grows.

Maybe you coughed or cleared your throat
maybe you blushed, maybe
in that instant before they opened the doors
you shielded your eyes from the blaze
maybe for a split second you thought about me

more accurately

wondered what you've done to suddenly
deserve the light pouring down on you.

Graced with intelligence, living
inside the head, we codify our days.
The merest events deepen into metaphors.

A word at the bright portal, even a thought
extends beyond itself; becomes a sign.

I say this in all sincerity:
I'd winter with the worms, truncated.
Surrender my last dime of heat—to you.

Happily rooted.
Happily pulsing below the surface, happily giving.
Asking little in return.

Hear me day & night from even the darkest caverns.
I'm the noisy sun, my summer stretched
to bursting.

What some might call the harbinger of life:
blushing poppies. An impressive but irregular
species of bird, airborne.

Read my lips.
Today I saw my heart on a billboard.

NOTES

"Nothing Happens, Nobody" is from *Waiting for Godot*, Grove Press, Inc. 1954.

In "The Unbearable Weight of Being," I have borrowed "ponders the insane root, the deadly nightshade, / the hemlock, the henbane that breedeth madness / or slow lykeness of sleepe" from an explanatory note on "the insane root," quoted in Act I, scene 3 of *The Tragedy of MacBeth*, D.C. Heath & Co., 1915. The line "the lucky blind untied to time" is paraphrased from *Godot* (56).

"For Walt, Frank et al., in Memoriam" is a nod to Walt Whitman and Frank O'Hara.

The epigraph in "After the Crematorium" is from *Nadja* by André Breton.

ABOUT THE AUTHOR

Carolyn Marie Souaid is a Montreal-based poet whose previous books have been shortlisted for the A.M. Klein Prize, the Mary Scorer Award, and the Pat Lowther Memorial Award. She is an editor, book reviewer and teacher, and the co-producer one of Montreal's most popular annual events —Circus of Words /Cirque des mots, a multidisciplinary, multilingual cabaret celebrating the "theatre" of poetry. Her work has been produced for CBC-Radio, and has been published nationally and internationally. She has appeared widely at literary festivals across Canada and in France.